AF406454

I WANT TO BE A
BIOCHEMIST

Written by
Jonathan Reule

Illustration
Chong Wey Ming

First paperback edition October 2023
ISBN 978-981-17359-9-8

Published by Unibino Pte. Ltd.
9 North Buona Vista Drive, #02-01 Metropolis Tower 1, Singapore 138588

www.unibino.com

Have you ever wondered what our bodies are made of? Yes, I'm sure you know about our skin, bones, and muscles, but do you know what makes up all of those elements at the cellular level? Well, if you look under a high-powered microscope, you'll see that our entire bodies are made up of tiny cells, constantly evolving and changing.

And this is where our Biochemists come into the picture. You see, these professionals work on cutting-edge research to find out how and why our cells, at a chemical level, react in biological ways.

But of course, this all began billions of years ago before there was any life on Earth! There are several theories floating around trying to explain the origins of life. Some people believe a bunch of matter exploded into existence one day, creating our universe and solar system in the process.

Others think that a god-like figure made everything in the universe, going so far as to design even the smallest details all the way down to the atomic level. But it's difficult for any one person to know for sure what the right answer is, especially since the world is way too old for anyone to have been there at the beginning of time.

When it comes to biological life on Earth, though, there are a few theories as to how it began. What science has shown us so far is that biological life seems to have started as tiny microbes found in 3.7 billion-year-old rocks! How those microbes got there is another mystery, but some believe they could've been attached to meteors falling from the sky, while others think they simply came to life due to a random occurrence.

What we do know is that these microscopic organisms soon began diving and evolving. Slowly over millions of years, these organisms started to change by growing a little bigger and a little more complex. In time they began adapting to Earth's environment. But as you can tell, Earth has a wide range of environments, which caused these microorganisms to evolve in a variety of ways.

Within each cell was a chemical reaction happening during their evolutions. But scientists don't know fully what these reactions were or how they came together to form life. But that's what happened. These microorganisms soon started to take shape into living beings.

Prehistoric fish began to fill up the oceans. These chemical reactions then caused some to take to the land, first evolving into amphibious creatures that could walk on land and live in the water. Over millions of years, these amphibious creatures had even more chemical changes occurring, which took away their flippers and gave them legs and lungs to live fully on land.

All of this happened thanks to the chemical reactions taking place at the cellular level. In time these land animals continued to evolve until one day, the first homo-sapien (human) came to life. It was from that point forward that we started observing our natural world and making informed predictions about it.

In no time, we realised our brains were one of our best sources of survival. This was when we started to have deeper questions about our existence on this earth and why we were different from other creatures. Of course, it would take many thousands of years before we dove into the scientific aspects of our evolution, but this is where the initial observation began.

It wasn't until the late BC period that we started to develop a more formalised approach to the study of our human anatomy and physiology.

It was during this time that several physicians, philosophers, and scientists began to seriously research how our bodies functioned. Physicians such as Hippocrates, often called the father of medicine, wrote extensively about his clinical observations throughout his lifetime. But perhaps one of his biggest contributions came from his theory that diseases were naturally occurring in our bodies rather than by some external spirit or god trying to plague us!

Around the same time, another Greek philosopher by the name of Democritus helped to popularise the concept of atomism. This was the belief that our bodies, and the entire world for that matter, were all made up of tiny components that we couldn't see with the naked eye. No one is certain who was the very first person to devise this theory, but it still supports the notion that our bodies are comprised of cells that release microscopic chemicals to keep us functioning.

As nice as these theories were, they only painted a broad picture of our understanding of how the human body worked for several centuries. It would take us quite a long time before we started to have a better grasp of our biology and the chemical processes happening within our systems. It wasn't until the 17th century that we first discovered stomach acid and its uses in our bodies.

This feat of research was first observed (or at least recorded) by army surgeon William Beaumont when he had a patient come into his surgery who had accidentally been shot through the stomach. The patient, Alexis St Martian, was expected to die from his wound, but in a miraculous turn, survived, leaving a hole in his abdomen that showed straight into his stomach. This was how Beaumont was able to see the stomach acid with his own eyes, along with having a better understanding of its role in digesting food.

This finding was pivotal for the field of biochemistry. It showed in a definitive way that our bodies had chemical reactions occurring inside while giving us insight into their biological effects. It was in the same century that enzymes were discovered and thoroughly studied, mainly to determine their impact on different elements.

Louis Pasteur, a French chemist, was instrumental in the discovery of enzymes. In the mid-1800s, he conducted experiments that demonstrated the role of enzymes in fermentation, a process in which microorganisms break down sugars to produce alcohol. Pasteur's work on enzymes helped to establish the field of biochemistry and laid the foundation for the study of metabolic processes. He also realised that enzymes were not merely byproducts of decay but were independent agents that played a crucial role in biochemical reactions.

As the study of enzymes progressed, other scientists joined the effort to understand the complex chemical reactions that take place in our bodies. One of the most significant findings over time was the identification and classification of biomolecules, which are essential components of living organisms. There are four main classifications of biomolecules: carbohydrates, lipids, nucleic acids, and proteins.

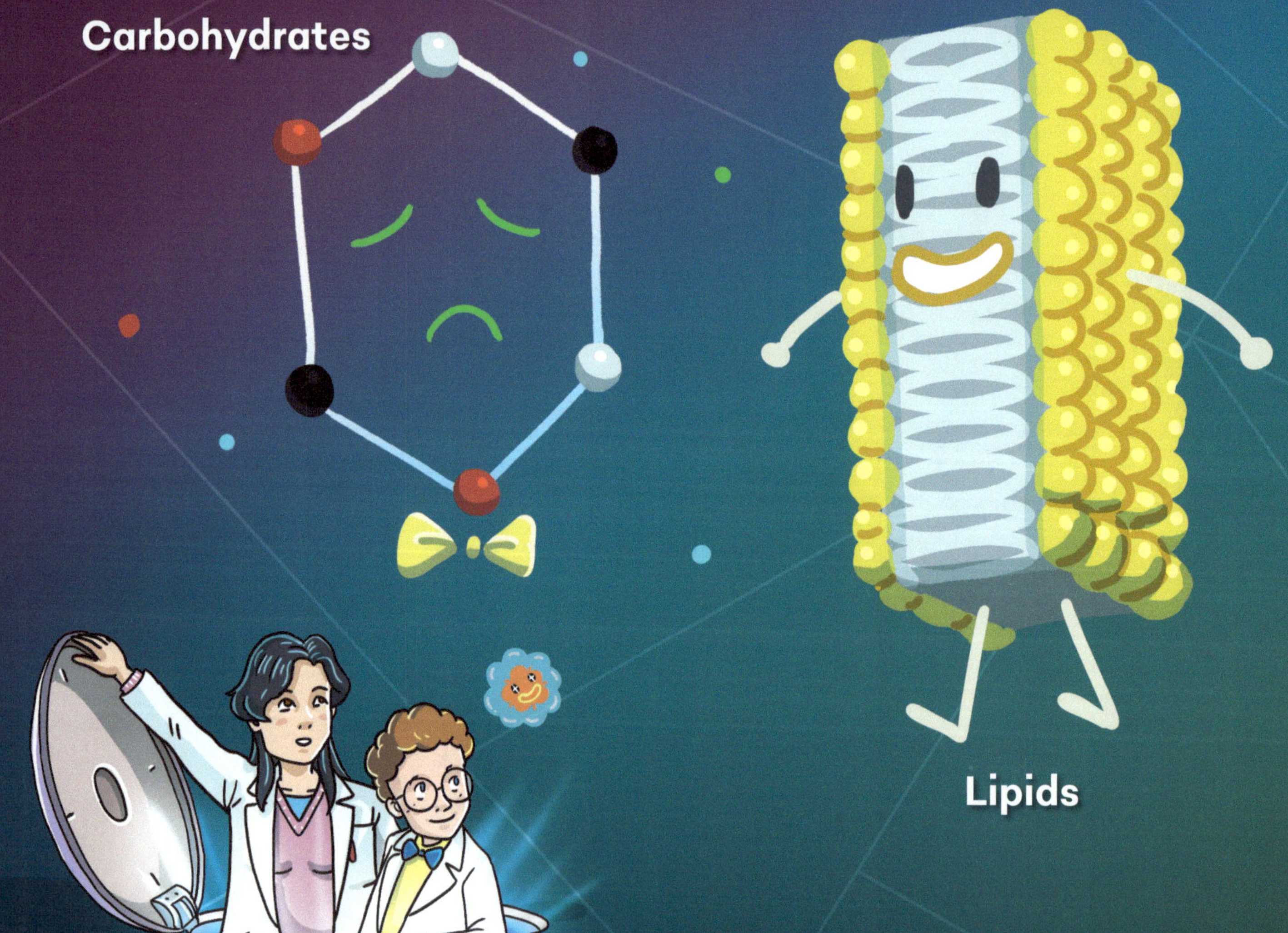

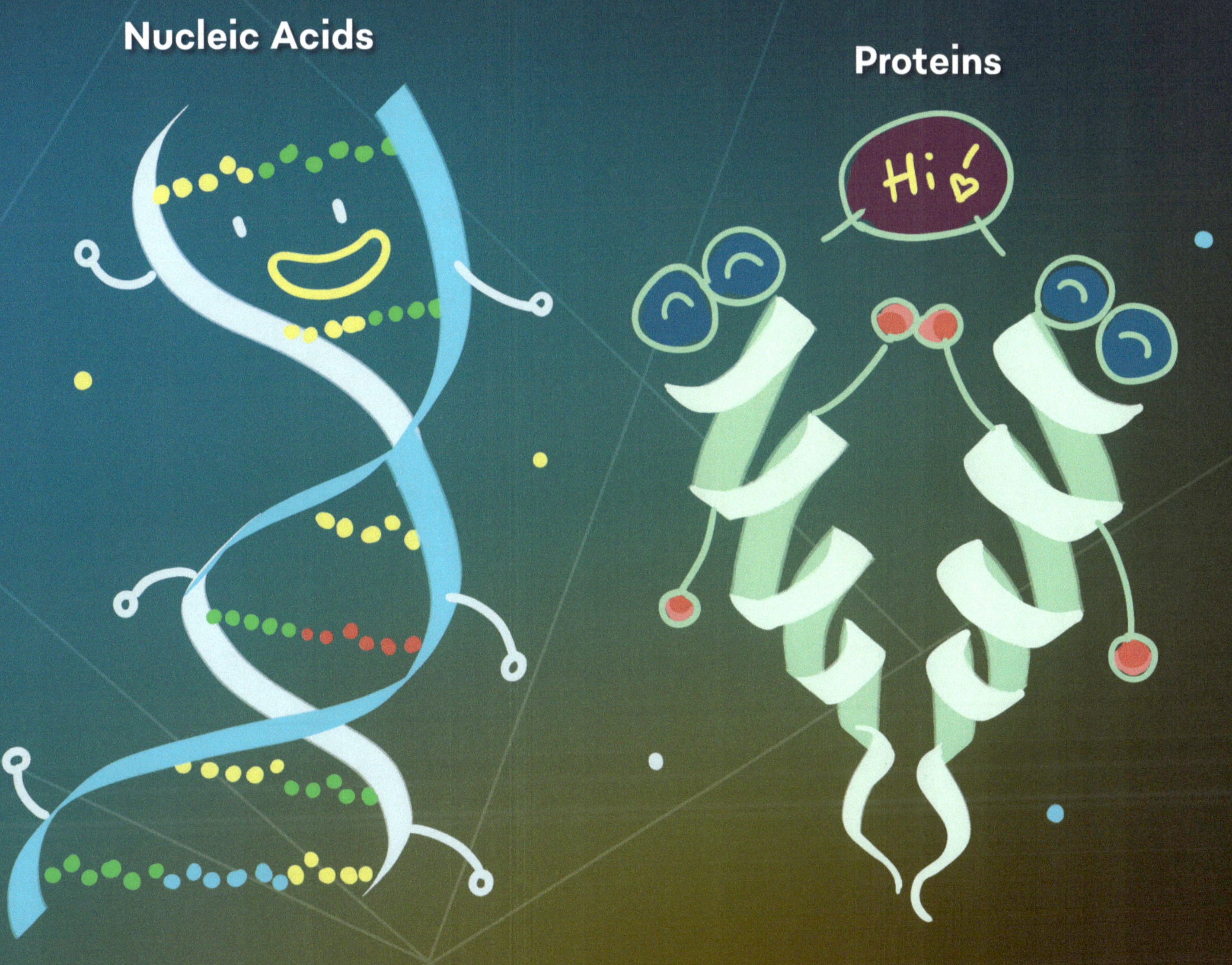

These molecules play a crucial role in various biochemical processes, including energy production, storage, and transmission of genetic information. The study of biomolecules and their functions has opened new avenues for understanding the complexity of living systems, paving the way for significant advancements in medicine, agriculture, and biotechnology.

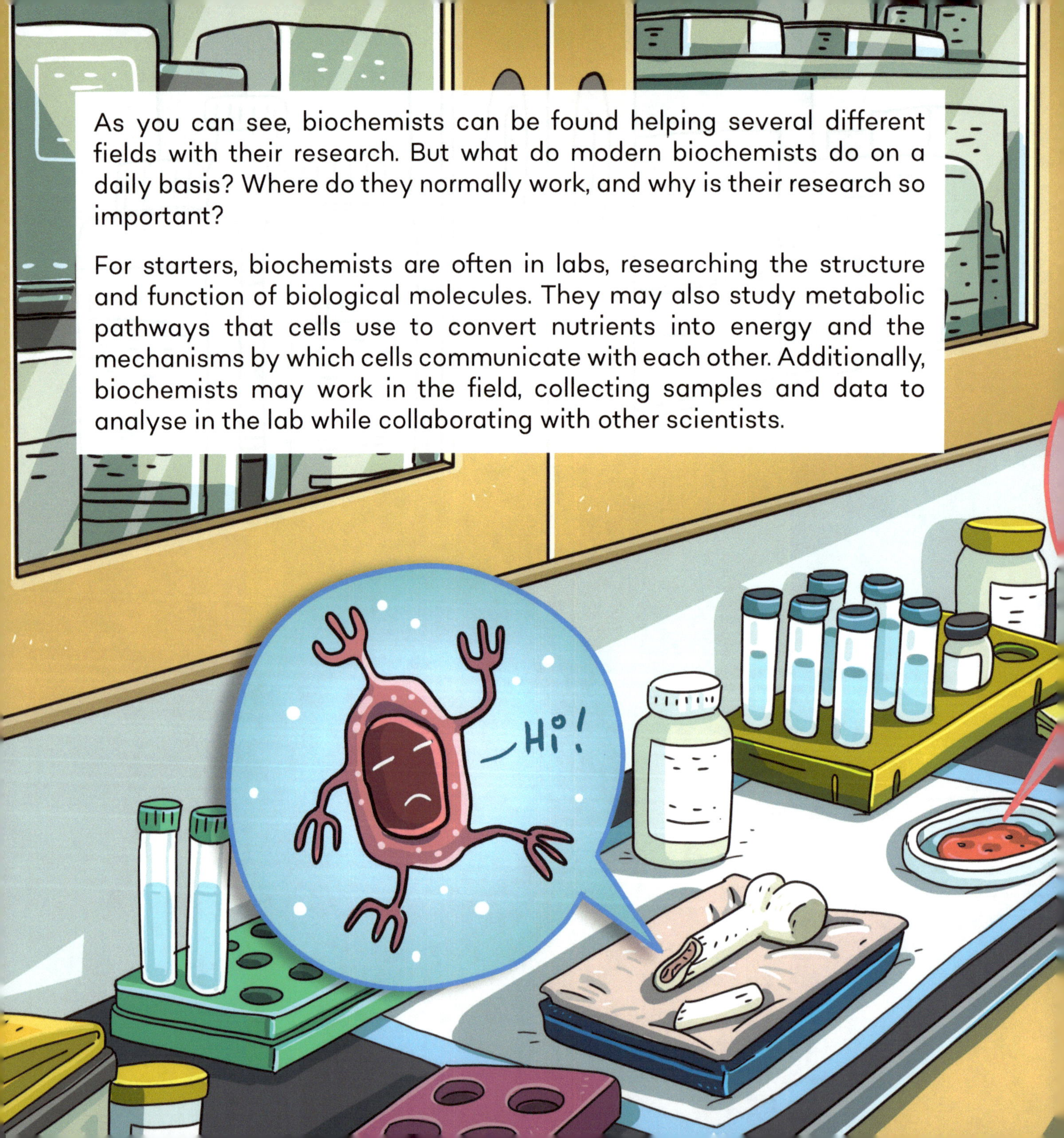

As you can see, biochemists can be found helping several different fields with their research. But what do modern biochemists do on a daily basis? Where do they normally work, and why is their research so important?

For starters, biochemists are often in labs, researching the structure and function of biological molecules. They may also study metabolic pathways that cells use to convert nutrients into energy and the mechanisms by which cells communicate with each other. Additionally, biochemists may work in the field, collecting samples and data to analyse in the lab while collaborating with other scientists.

Hi!
Hi!

But what can they discover from their studies? Well, as we mentioned earlier, they can help a whole host of different fields. Take the medical field, for example. It takes a team of biochemists to make drugs and medications. By observing biochemical reactions, they can determine how to make drugs that will help relieve painful symptoms or change the way our bodies work.

In addition to drug development, biochemists play a critical role in diagnosing and treating diseases. They can analyse the chemical composition of bodily fluids and tissues to detect abnormalities and monitor disease progression. Biochemists can also develop new diagnostic tools and techniques, such as molecular imaging, that allow doctors to visualise and track diseases in real time!

In agriculture, biochemists work to develop new plant varieties with improved yields and resistance to pests and diseases. They also study the biochemical pathways involved in plant growth and development. In food science, biochemists study the nutritional value of food and develop new food products with enhanced nutrition and taste.

Continuing on this path, biochemists also play a key role in environmental and energy-related fields. In environmental science, biochemists study the effects of pollutants on ecosystems and develop methods for bioremediation (the process of breaking down pollutants). They also research the biochemical pathways involved in biogeochemical (bio-geo-chemical) cycles, such as the carbon and nitrogen cycles that occur in soil.

Learning all of this information may have you wondering now what it takes to be a biochemist. As you can probably tell, a person needs to have a great passion for learning about microorganisms, along with other microscopic chemicals. This means that you should be prepared to stay in a lab looking through microscopes while making calculations for all of your findings.

To become a professional biochemist, a strong foundation in biology and chemistry is essential. This involves studying diligently at university and then applying to either a PhD program in biochemistry or a specialised master's program. Most practising biochemists hold at least a master's degree in the field.

After acquiring an advanced degree, you can decide what type of Biochemist you'd like to be. There are four main branches that study different biological and chemical organisms. The first is Enzymology, the study of different enzymes and their impact on biological matter. The second is the study of Metabolism and how that chemical process digests foods and turns it into energy for our bodies.

The third is Plant biochemistry, a fascinating field that focuses on the chemical processes taking place within plants. By studying the interactions between plants and their environments, plant biochemists seek to understand how plants grow, reproduce, and respond to stress. And the fourth is Animal biochemistry which studies how animals maintain their biological functions, including metabolism, cell signalling, and protein synthesis.

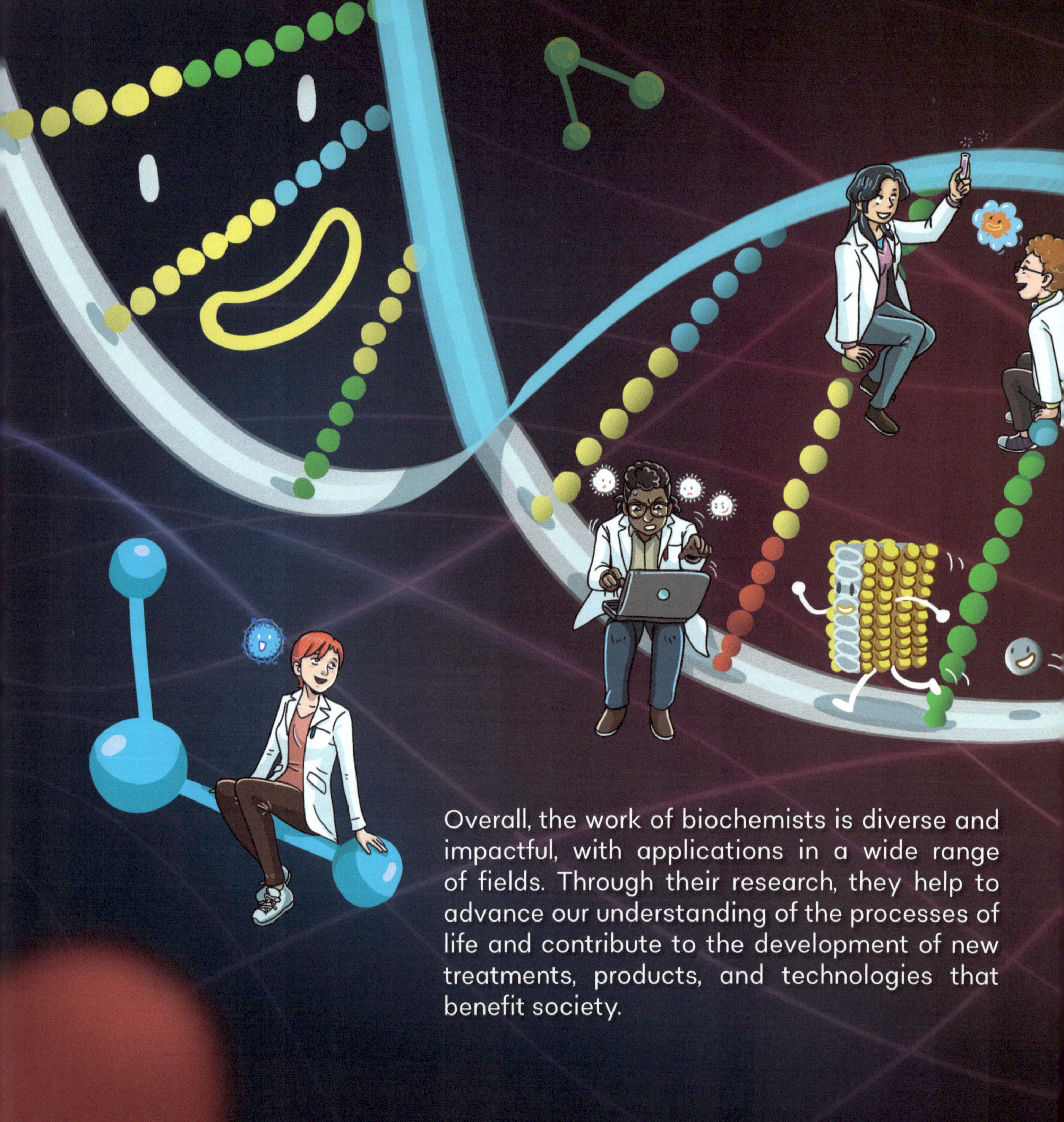

Overall, the work of biochemists is diverse and impactful, with applications in a wide range of fields. Through their research, they help to advance our understanding of the processes of life and contribute to the development of new treatments, products, and technologies that benefit society.

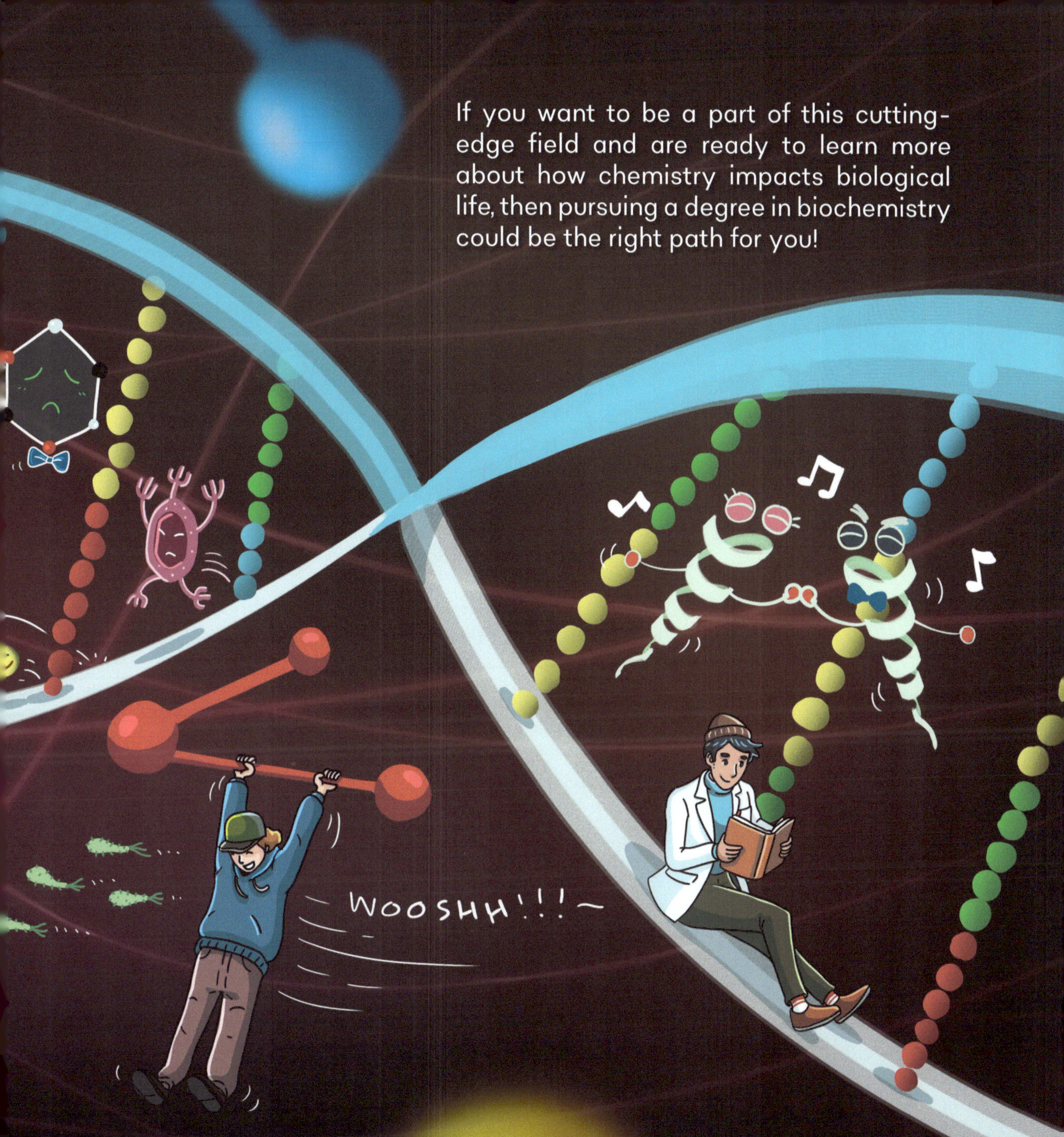

If you want to be a part of this cutting-edge field and are ready to learn more about how chemistry impacts biological life, then pursuing a degree in biochemistry could be the right path for you!
WOOSHH!!!~

My Inspiration

As a parent in this ever-changing world, it can sometimes feel overwhelming when it comes to our children's futures. New technologies seem to be arising almost every day, and with so many innovations, it creates unique professions which many of us wouldn't have dreamed to be necessary only a few years ago. Which to me is a good thing. Because with so much variety, my children can have the opportunity to pick a career that will fit their personalities and build upon their strengths. As you may imagine, this desire within me to provide my children with the resources they needed to thrive, led me to search out books that would be easy enough for them to understand while teaching them about various professions.

Shubhi Saxena
Founder, Unibino

Only, I found that these books were few and far between. Even if I could find a book about a certain profession geared towards young readers, I found them sparse inside and limited to only certain careers that may not fit my children's abilities. This is when I came up with the idea to write my own children's books, teaching them about all the various careers in the modern world. After months of researching different professions and learning more than I ever expected, I quickly realised this was going to be a bigger project than I first anticipated. I dove into the histories of these professions, discovering links to the past, and why these professions were now so important.

Ultimately my goal was to offer my children options, to show them that there is no one set path for everyone. But in this, I stumbled upon something bigger. I wanted to share this with future generations. To share with all children and parents about these careers, to help spark curiosity, and to instil a passion for the future. Everyone has special talents and abilities, and I hope that this series will be able to offer clarity and inspiration to children around the world. Because at the end of the day, it's never too early to start dreaming and never too late to take action. With this, I hope you enjoy this series and that your young ones become the best versions of themselves as they can achieve.